★American Girl®
Coloring Journal

weldon**owen**

Kaya is a member of the Nimíipuu tribe, a Native American people who are now known as Nez Perce. She loves horses and works hard to earn the trust of her young filly, Steps High. Kaya looks to her elders and the strong women in her village as she learns to become a leader for her people.

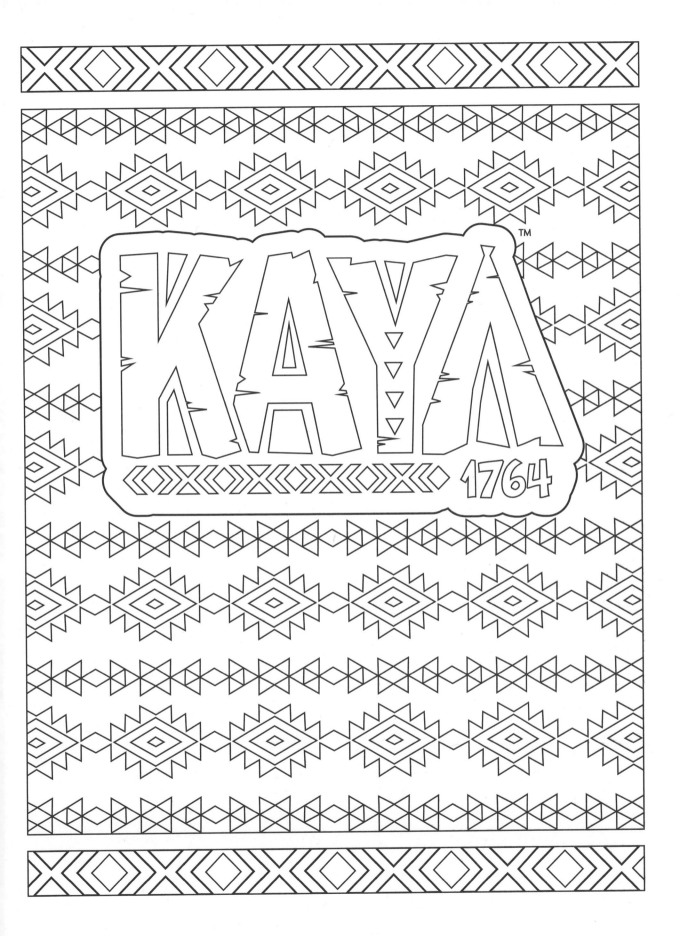

The Shape of Your World

Kaya and her people create beautiful geometric designs on hats, woven baskets, and parfleches (storage envelopes). The zig zag pattern is in honor of the mountains where the Nez Perce live. What shapes would you draw to represent your home or neighborhood? Create a pattern with those shapes below.

Meditation Bracelet

The Nez Perce wear necklaces and chokers made from beads and other materials like dyed porcupine quills. You can make your own jewelry from materials found at any craft store. Homemade jewelry is fashionable, and making it can be a calming activity that provides focus and peace of mind. Follow the instructions below to make a calming beaded bracelet of your own.

Start with an elastic cord. It should be long enough to wrap around your wrist one and a half times so you have enough excess material to tie into a knot when you are done.

Fold a piece of tape over one end of the elastic to keep the beads from falling off.

Select your beads. They can be either plastic, wood, glass, or stone. (For an elastic string, plastic generally works best.)

Lay your beads out in a row to determine the order of the beads, then slide each bead onto the elastic until your bracelet is the perfect length for your wrist.

Once all the beads are on the elastic, tie the ends together and put a dab of glue on the knot to keep it in place. Wait until the glue dries before putting the bracelet on your wrist.

Whenever you feel upset, use the beads on the bracelet to calm yourself. Take a breath each time you touch a bead as you work your way around the circle.

With each bead, think of one thing that you are grateful for.

Once you reach the final bead, close your eyes and take one final deep, cleansing breath.

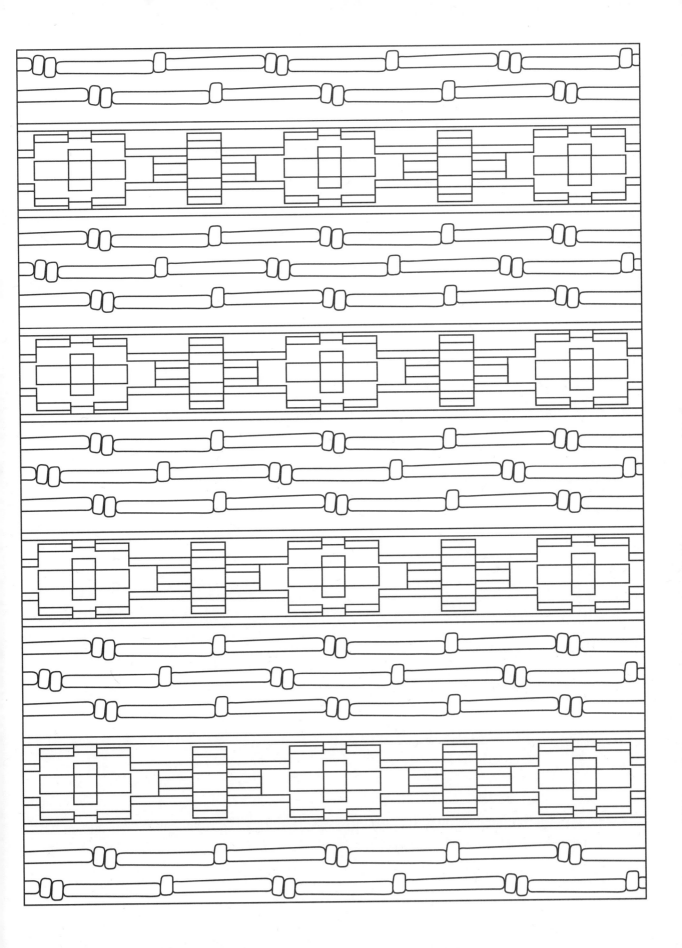

Felicity Merriman lives in Williamsburg, Virginia, during the American Revolution. She isn't fond of "sitting down kinds of things" like stitchery and writing. She'd much rather be outside, and she loves anything to do with horses!

Host a Tea Party

Small gatherings can be a wonderful way to get to know people better. Imagine you are the host of your own tea party and you can invite anyone in the world to be your guests, either living or dead. Who would you invite? What questions would you ask them?

Calming Techniques

Felicity is fond of a spirited horse whom she names Penny because of her copper-colored coat. To calm the horse and earn her trust, Felicity must sit still and be patient—two things she is normally not good at.

What are some of the ways you calm yourself when you're feeling stressed? Here are a few things you can do when you're feeling agitated.

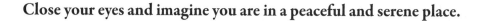

Close your eyes and imagine you are in a peaceful and serene place.

Repeat a phrase as a mantra like "I am calm."

Count to 10.

Take a deep breath and release it slowly. Repeat two more times.

**Take a walk in nature or around your neighborhood.
Focus on what you see, hear, and smell.**

Ride a bike or go roller-skating.

Take a hot bath or a cool shower.

Pick a spot in your house as your special place. Make it comfortable with pillows, stuffed animals, or other items that relax you. Rest there until you feel less anxious.

Josefina Montoya is growing up in New Mexico in 1824, when Spanish, Mexican, and Native American people share the land. Josefina is brave enough to embrace new ideas while holding on to what is precious from her past.

Animal Guide

Josefina raises a baby goat as a pet. She names the goat *Sombrita*—which means little shadow—because the little goat follows her everywhere. If you have a pet or know someone who does, sit with the animal for a while and get to know it better by answering these questions.

Describe what the animal looks like. What colors or patterns are on its body?

_____

_____

_____

Does it make any noise? What does it sound like when it is resting quietly? What does it sound like when it is active or playing?

_____

_____

_____

What does it feel like? (If the animal isn't your pet, only touch an animal when you have permission from the owner.)

_____

_____

_____

Describe its scent. What does it smell like?

_____

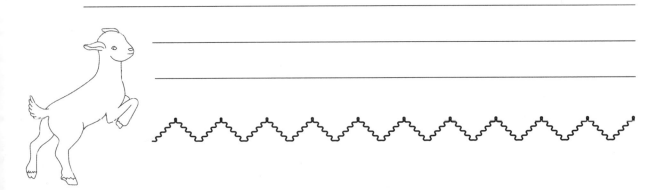

_____

_____

The Patterns Around You

When Josefina learns to weave blankets, she creates designs inspired by the mountains, valleys, and streams around her home. There are patterns in everything around you, from the wood on a table and the keys on a keyboard, to the loops in your fingerprints and the feathers on a bird. Explore the space around you, and draw some of the patterns you find below.

Kirsten Larson and her family make a long journey from Sweden to start a new life in America in the nineteenth century. After months on a cramped ship, Kirsten arrives at a small farm on the edge of the wide-open frontier. It's her new home!

Find Your Home

Kirsten's family of five move into a tiny log cabin with just one room. It's special because it's their first home in America. It's nice to have a special place to go to be alone with your thoughts. If you could set up a truly special space for yourself, where would it be? What items would you put in it? Draw up your plans for your own special place below.

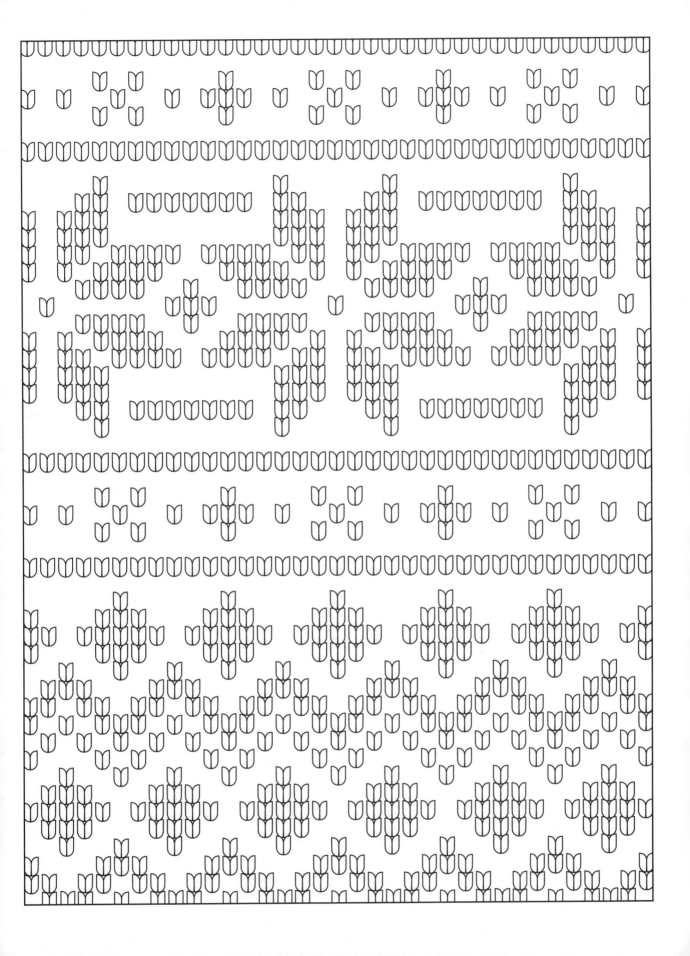

Memory Quilt

Kirsten loves sewing with her school friends at recess. Their teacher even shows them how to make a quilt. Today, people make memory quilts by sewing together different fabrics from personal items that mean something to them, like a favorite shirt they have outgrown or a handkerchief that belonged to a relative. You don't have to know how to sew to create a memory quilt. You can draw it on the page below.

Find four pieces of cloth that mean something special to you. These can be your favorite outfit or something a family member wore to a special occasion. Choose a section of that fabric for your quilt. Draw the pattern from that fabric in one of the squares below. Repeat until you've filled each square and you will have your quilt.

Addy Walker escapes slavery during the Civil War and travels north to freedom. She and her mother settle in Philadelphia, where Addy attends school for the first time. Freedom isn't always what Addy expected, and she misses her father, brother, and sister terribly. Addy holds love and hope in her heart until her whole family is reunited.

In Your Heart

Addy had to be brave and determined to escape slavery. She put her family's needs before her own and even gave her beloved rag doll, Janie, to her baby sister, Esther, so she would always keep Addy in her heart. What character traits help you face challenges? Choose what words describe you best from the list below or add your own words. Place them in the heart in order of how important you consider them to be. Place the traits of lesser importance at the bottom of the heart, with the most important traits filling the lines at the top of the heart.

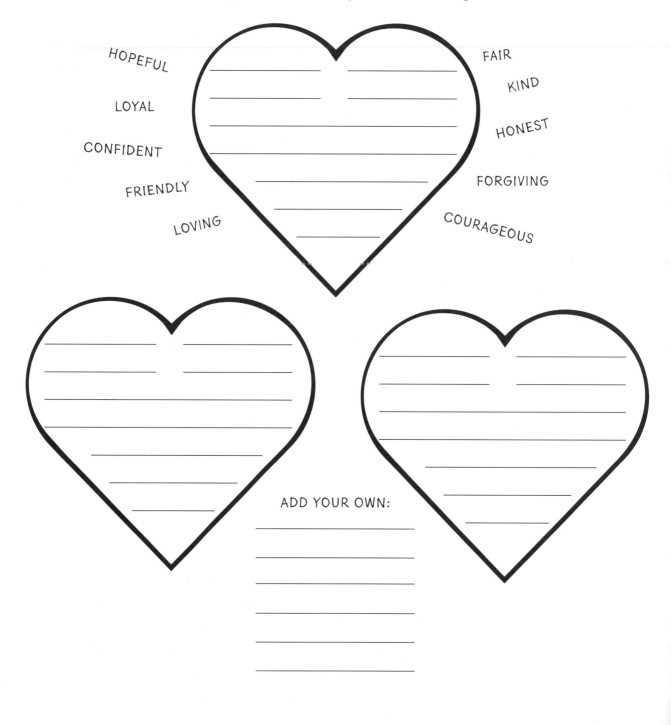

HOPEFUL

LOYAL

CONFIDENT

FRIENDLY

LOVING

FAIR

KIND

HONEST

FORGIVING

COURAGEOUS

ADD YOUR OWN:

Personal Treasures

Addy wears a cowrie-shell necklace that had been passed down to her from her great-grandmother. Do you have any items that belonged to someone else in your family? Do you have any items that you'd want to pass to your children someday? Draw a picture of either one below, and then write about why the item is meaningful.

_____

_____

_____

_____

_____

Rebecca Rubin is growing up in 1914 in a Jewish immigrant neighborhood in New York City. Rebecca loves to sing along to the phonograph and perform for an audience. She dreams of being an actress. As a first generation American, she often finds that her interests, like her dreams of becoming a movie star, are at odds with her family's beliefs and traditions. Rebecca learns that she can pursue her dreams while still honoring her heritage.

Movie Night

Rebecca visits her cousin Max at a movie studio and she learns how movies are made. Films can teach us a lot about the world around us and about people who are different from us. Try new experiences with a mindful movie night. Choose a movie from the list below to watch on your own or to share with the special people in your life.

WATCH A MOVIE THAT . . .

. . . you don't think you're going to like.

. . . you haven't watched since you were really young.

. . . you saw years ago and hated at the time.

. . . a friend your own age recommended.

. . . an older friend or family member recommended.

. . . was filmed in black and white.

. . . has subtitles.

. . . is really long.

. . . is really short.

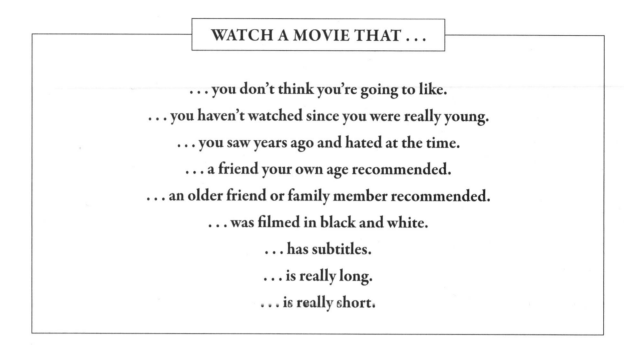

MOVIES WATCHED . . .

_____

_____

_____

_____

_____

_____

_____

_____

Who Are You?

Rebecca has a set of nesting dolls that belonged to her mother back in Russia, so they are a symbol of her family's heritage. What are some of the symbols from your heritage? Feel free to define your heritage however you like, and draw those images below.

Kit Kittredge's family goes from rich to poor overnight during the Great Depression. Kit wants to help her family keep their house and pay the bills, and she is willing to give up dance lessons and other luxuries to do so. With her strong, resourceful spirit, Kit believes that no problem is too big to tackle.

Growing Your Garden

To save money, Kit's family starts a vegetable garden in their backyard. It is extra work for everyone, but it helps feed the family. Gardening can also be a fun and relaxing activity. What would you grow in your garden? Draw it below.

Read All About It

Kit loves making a newspaper for her dad, reporting on everything that happens at home while he's at work. What stories in your own home or neighborhood are newsworthy events? Use the space below to list the topics you'd write about if you started your own newspaper.

Nanea Mitchell is nine years old when Japan attacks Pearl Harbor, the naval base in Hawaii where her father works. This act leads the United States to enter World War II. Island life changes dramatically for Nanea and her family. She is determined to do what she can to help her neighbors and support the servicemen fighting the war. She makes food for aid workers, performs hula for wounded soldiers, and helps organize a bottle drive for the Red Cross.

Aloha Spirit

The war brings new chores for Nanea and new challenges to Hawaii. Nanea and her family and friends face them with the spirit of aloha: kindness, respect, and understanding. Think of what those words mean to you. Use words or pictures to represent those concepts below.

KINDNESS

RESPECT

UNDERSTANDING

Flower Power

A tropical flower lei (pronounced *lay*) is one of the most widely recognized symbols of Hawaii. A lei is worn around the neck like a necklace. It can be given as a gift or worn at weddings, birthday parties, or graduations, but it can also be part of an everyday wardrobe.

Nanea's grandmother teaches her how to make a lei as part of her hula lessons because the colors and materials of a lei help tell the story of the dance. Leis can be made from flowers, leaves, feathers, shells, or nuts. Any kind of flowers or other natural materials can be used to make a lei, but some items carry special messages.

Plumeria flowers represent new beginnings.

Purple orchids send a message of greeting and appreciation.

Hawaiian hibiscus are a symbol of joyfulness and beauty.

Golden ilima signify love.

Bird of Paradise flowers represent freedom.

Green maile ti leaves are a sign of respect or admiration.

Kukui nuts show appreciation.

Molly McIntire is also growing up during World War II. She's used to "fighting on the home front" with scrap drives, victory gardens, and rationing. She misses her father, a doctor who is in far-away England helping wounded soldiers. Molly does her red, white, and blue best to be a patriotic citizen.

You've Got the Look

Molly tries to change her appearance to show her father that she has grown up while he was away. But when he returns, she finds that he's most grateful to see her exactly as she has always been, proving that a "new" Molly wasn't necessary. Take a good look at yourself in a mirror. Choose three things that you like most about yourself. Draw a self-portrait below, focusing on the things you like the most. (It doesn't matter if you're not an artist. Just have fun with it.)

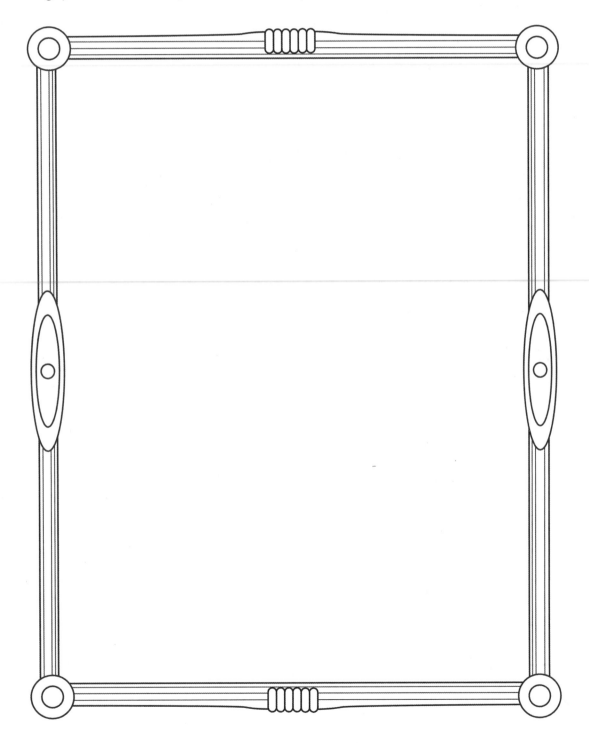

Someone Special

Molly has a number of friends. She's known some of them, like Linda and Susan, her whole life. Others, like Emily, who comes from England to stay with the McIntires, are new friends. Do you have a special person you can talk to about anything? What are some of the things you have in common? Why do you consider them special? Write about that person below.

Maryellen Larkin is growing up in the suburbs during the 1950s. She has a one-of-a-kind mind full of big, imaginative ideas, and she longs to stand out. But in a family with five noisy siblings, she often gets lost in the shuffle.

Invention Inspiration

Maryellen is the only girl in her school's science club. She has a great idea for inventing a flying machine! Have you ever wanted to invent something? Imagine an invention that would make life easier for yourself or someone you know. Draw up your plans for that invention in the space below.

Conversation Starters

TV dinners were popular in the 1950s. The frozen food contained a complete meal in a tin-foil tray that just had to be popped into the oven to heat. Many families started eating dinner on trays in their living rooms while they watched television. When they went out for casual meals, people often went to diners, which gained popularity as families moved out of cities and into the expanding suburbs.

Whether you're eating at home or out on the town, mealtime is always a good opportunity for meaningful conversations. Sometimes, it can be difficult to get a discussion started, so it helps to come armed with a few conversation starters. Write some interesting questions or topics you can use to jump start a conversation below.

Melody Ellison is growing up during the civil rights movement of the 1960s. She's learning about the different ways Black people are fighting for equal rights. When Melody experiences discrimination for herself, she decides to stand up and speak out about civil rights, too.

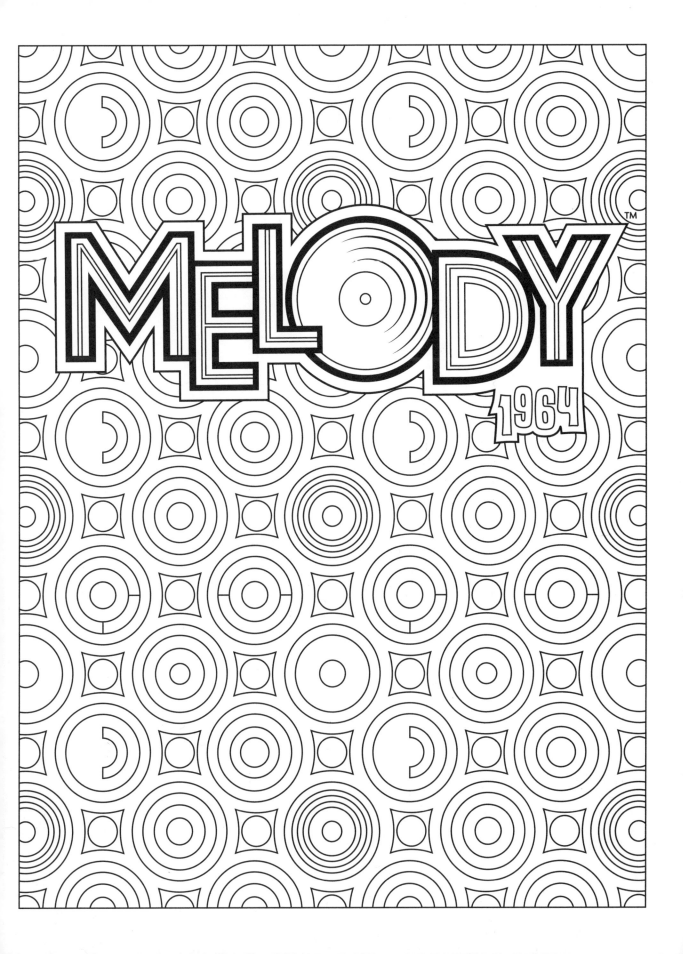

The Music in You

Music plays a significant role in Melody's life. She performs in the children's choir in her church and even sings backup when her brother records a song he wrote. Sometimes, Melody uses songs to share a particular message, but music can say a lot even when there are no words to sing. Choose a piece of music that has no lyrics. Close your eyes and listen to the song all the way until the end. Think of how the music makes you feel. Then draw a picture inspired by that music and the feelings it evokes in you below.

A Sign of Protest

When Melody and her brother are accused of shoplifting, they boycott the store as a form of protest. They aren't the only Black people who have been treated unfairly there, so Melody joins a picket line in front of the store. She makes a sign that says "Support Our Boycott."

Throughout the civil rights movement, people made signs, like those on the opposite page. What issues would you fight for or against? Create your own protest signs to express your point of view for that issue below.

Julie Albright is a child of the 1970s, a time when women and girls began to seek equal rights with men and boys. Julie starts a petition to play on the boys' basketball team and she also becomes the first fifth grader to run for student body president at school. Julie has big ideas for how to make the school a better place for every student!

Presidential Platform

When Julie runs for student body president, her platform—her message about the improvements she wants to make—begins with changing the detention system. Have you ever run for office in your school or another organization? If you were going to run for president of something—your school, a club, the country—what would your platform be? Write it below.

Reuse and Upcycle

Julie's mother asserts her independence by starting her own business. Gladrags is a store that sells reused items, like handmade purses made out of worn-out blue jeans.

Today, the act of making something useful out of items other people would consider junk is called upcycling. You can make jewelry from discarded board games, dresses out of old T-shirts, and pillows from torn beach towels. Next time you're about to throw out an article of clothing, an unused toy, or any items you can no longer use, think of ways to turn that trash into something new and better first. Draw your plans for upcycling that item below.

Courtney Moore lives in California in the 1980s. She watches music videos on MTV after school, rents movies on the weekends, and plays video games at the arcade whenever she can. Courtney's one of the best gamers around, but she wishes there were more female characters. That's why she makes up her own superhero: Crystal Starshooter.

Music Mix

Making a mixtape was a popular activity in the 1980s. Kids would record their favorite songs from the radio or an album onto one cassette tape. Mixtapes were popular gifts for friends. Today, we make playlists instead, which is a lot easier than making a mixtape.

Playlists can help you set a mood. They are great to use when you're exercising, studying, hanging out with friends, or relaxing at the end of the day. Which songs would you choose for each activity?

Workout mix

Hanging out with friends

Dancing by myself

Homework tunes

Taking a nature walk

Singing out loud when no one else is around

Peaceful meditation

Labyrinth

Video games rose in popularity in the 1980s as technology grew more advanced. Because graphics were still simple, game play was often about guiding a character through a maze.

A maze can be confusing, with all its twists and turns, but a walking labyrinth is a different experience. This kind of maze is usually a circular path in the ground that contains only one path. People use them to calm themselves and be inspired as they walk to the center of the path. If you don't have a walking labyrinth in your town, grab a pencil and slowly follow the path below. Don't rush. Take your time getting to the center.

weldon**owen**

PO Box 3088
San Rafael, CA 94912
www.weldonowen.com

Library of Congress Cataloging-in-Publication Data available.

ISBN: 978-1-68188-525-4

CEO: Raoul Goff
Publisher: Roger Shaw
VP of Licensing and Partnerships: Vanessa Lopez
VP of Creative: Chrissy Kwasnik
VP of Manufacturing: Alix Nicholaeff
Associate Publisher: Sara Miller
Art Director: Stuart Smith
Designer: Leah Lauer
Senior Editor: Paul Puditis
Editorial Assistant: Elizabeth Ovieda
Managing Editor: Vicki Jaeger
Senior Production Editor: Jennifer Bentham
Production Manager: Sam Taylor
Senior Production Manager, Subsidiary Rights: Lina s Palma

Illustrations by: Artful Doodlers
Additional art: P.78 tash19/shutterstock.com

ROOTS of PEACE   REPLANTED PAPER

Insight Editions, in association with Roots of Peace, will plant two trees for each tree used in the
manufacturing of this book. Roots of Peace is an internationally renowned humanitarian organization dedicated to eradicating land mines worldwide and converting war-torn lands into productive
farms and wildlife habitats. Roots of Peace will plant two million fruit and nut trees in Afghanistan
and provide farmers there with the skills and support necessary for sustainable land use.

Manufactured in Turkey

10 9 8 7 6 5 4 3 2 1